EARTH MATERIALS AND SYSTEMS

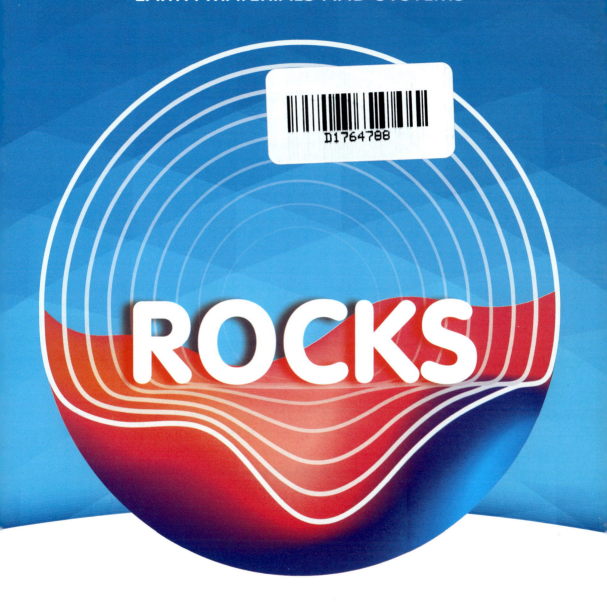

ROCKS

by Tamra B. Orr

Raintree is an imprint of Capstone Global Library Limited, a company incorporated in England and Wales having its registered office at 264 Banbury Road, Oxford, OX2 7DY – Registered company number: 6695582

www.raintree.co.uk
myorders@raintree.co.uk

Edited by Charly Haley
Designed by Jake Nordby
Original illustrations © Capstone Global Library Limited 2022
Production by Joshua Olson
Originated by Capstone Global Library Ltd
Printed and bound in India

978 1 3982 0410 2 (hardback)
978 1 3982 0409 6 (paperback)

British Library Cataloguing in Publication Data
A full catalogue record for this book is available from the British Library.

Acknowledgements
We would like to thank the following for permission to reproduce photographs: iStockphoto: abadonian, 10, Francois Boudrias, 9, goncharovaia, 25, Ilia Bystrov, 14, JacobH, 13, noblige, 5, Siobhan_Fraser, 28, slavemotion, 17, t-lorien, 18; Shutterstock Images: Clara Bastian, 21, Hecos, 27, Randy McVeigh, 26, Red Tiger, 23, robert cicchetti, 6, superoke, cover, Yuriy Buyvol, 7. Design elements: Shutterstock Images.

Every effort has been made to contact copyright holders of material reproduced in this book. Any omissions will be rectified in subsequent printings if notice is given to the publisher.

CONTE

What are rocks? 4

How do rocks form? 8

Where are rocks found? 16

Why are rocks important? 24

Glossary 30

Find out more 31

Index... 32

Words in **bold** are in the glossary.

What are rocks?

Rocks are all around us. You can see them outside. Small stones on the pavement are rocks. Large boulders on mountains are rocks too. Many rocks are underground.

Some rocks are smooth. Others are rough. Rocks are all shapes and sizes. Wind and water can change a rock's shape over time.

All rocks are made of at least one **mineral**. Most rocks are made of more than one mineral. Minerals are things in nature that are not alive.

A rock's colour comes from its minerals. Rocks made from different minerals are different colours.

How do rocks form?

There are three types of rocks. One type is called igneous rock. Igneous rocks are made from melted rock that has cooled. Melted rock is deep underground. It is called **magma**. It is very hot.

This melted rock comes out of **volcanoes** as **lava**. The lava flows across the ground. The lava cools as it moves. It becomes hard rock. This is called igneous rock.

Igneous rocks

Some igneous rocks are smooth and shiny. They are made when lava cools quickly. Other igneous rocks are rough. They are made when lava cools slowly.

Igneous rocks also form when magma cools underground. These rocks are called **granite**.

A second type of rock is called sedimentary rock. These are rocks made from small pieces such as sand or pebbles.

Sedimentary rocks are made when these pieces get buried. The small pieces press together. They become hard rock. Then the rock gets buried under more small pieces. The new pieces harden. They form a new **layer**.

The rock keeps getting buried. More layers form. The rock gets bigger. This happens over millions of years.

Dead plants and animals can help to form sedimentary rocks too. Dead animals and plants break down and become part of the rocks.

The third type of rock is called metamorphic rock. These rocks are made from other rocks.

Rocks change when they get very hot. This happens to rocks that are buried deep within Earth. Buried rocks also change when the ground pushes down on them. These changes make new minerals in the rocks. The rocks become metamorphic rocks. These changes happen over millions of years.

Where are rocks found?

Rocks are everywhere. Most rocks that people see are sedimentary rocks. These rocks are often found near water. Moving water in rivers or oceans breaks rocks into small pieces. These pieces eventually form sedimentary rocks.

These rocks are found in deserts too. Wind blows fast across flat desert land. This wind hits rocks. It breaks them into pieces over time. The pieces form sedimentary rocks.

People sometimes use machines to get metamorphic rocks out of mountains.

People can also find metamorphic rocks. These rocks form deep underground. But they can get pushed above ground over time.

People usually find these rocks near mountains. Mountains are in places where the ground moves a lot. This happens slowly. The moving soil pushes on buried rocks. This makes metamorphic rocks.

Igneous rocks can be found near volcanoes. But many are in the ground. These rocks make up most of the rocks in Earth's **crust**. Earth has many layers underground. Earth's crust is the top layer. It is the layer we walk on. Most of the ocean floor is also made of these rocks.

Rocks are always changing. The changes happen very slowly over millions of years. Rocks change into different types of rocks. This is called the rock cycle.

Rocks form deep underground. They heat and cool. They break or bend. They are pushed above ground. Rain and wind move them. Some break into small pieces. The pieces get buried and harden. All of these things change rocks. Any rock can change into a different type of rock.

Why are rocks important?

We use rocks for many different things. Some rocks are used to make buildings. Bricks are made of rocks. The concrete in pavements is made of rocks too.

Many things that we use every day are made of rocks. Rocks are used to make some of the plates and bowls that we use. An igneous rock called pumice is used in the making of denim jeans. This rock is rubbed on fabric. It makes the fabric look like the jeans we wear.

Rocks make homes for many plants and animals. Some things live only on mountains. They would not have homes without these rocky places.

Rocks also help feed plants. The minerals in rocks get into soil. Minerals help plants grow.

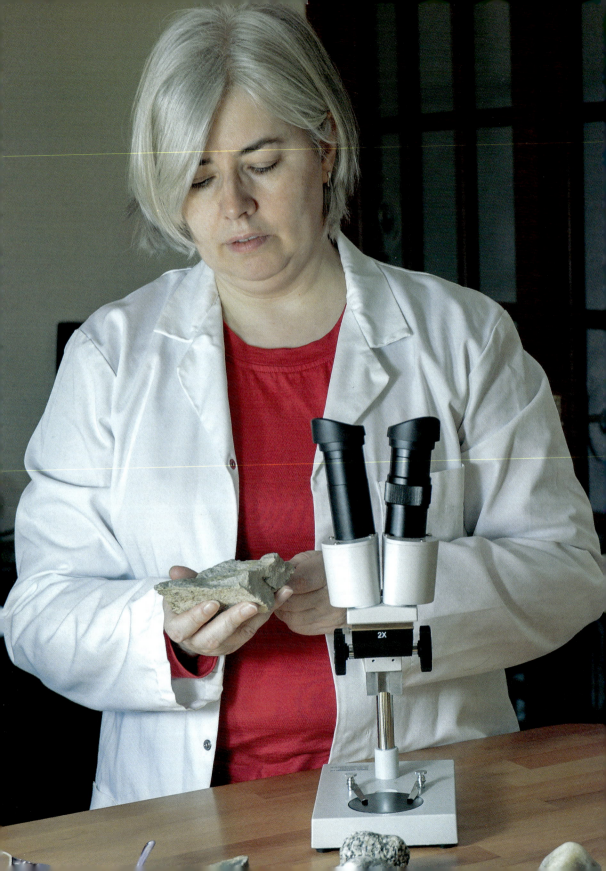

Rocks can help us learn about the past. Scientists study rocks. They learn about what Earth was like long ago. Rocks can show scientists if a place once had a volcano. Rocks can show if a place was once underwater.

We see rocks around us every day. Rocks are always slowly changing. They come in many forms, and many living things use them. Rocks help us learn about Earth.

Glossary

crust top layer of Earth

granite hard igneous rock used in buildings

lava hot liquid rock that comes out of a volcano

layer thickness of something that lies on or under something else

magma melted rock found beneath Earth's surface; magma flows as lava out of volcanoes and becomes igneous rock when it cools

mineral solid substance in the ground made by nature that is not a plant or animal; minerals are found in rocks and soil

volcano mountain that can erupt to let out lava

Find out more

Books

Earth (DKfindout!), DK (DK Children, 2017)

Rocks (Rock On!), Chris Oxlade (Raintree, 2017)

Rocks and Minerals (Eyewitness Workbooks),
DK (DK Children, 2020)

Websites

**www.bbc.co.uk/bitesize/topics/z9bbkqt/articles/
zsgkdmn**

Learn more about rocks and their properties.

www.dkfindout.com/uk/earth/rock-cycle

Find out more about the rock cycle.

Index

animals 12, 26

boulders 4
buildings 24

deserts 16

granite 11

igneous rocks 8, 11, 20, 24

lava 8, 11

magma 8, 11
metamorphic rocks 15, 19

minerals 7, 15, 27
mountains 4, 19, 26

pavements 4, 24
pebbles 11
plants 12, 26, 27
pumice 24

sand 11
scientists 29
sedimentary rocks 11, 12, 16

volcanoes 8, 20, 29

water 4, 16, 29
wind 4, 16, 22